Beemer's Adventures

Beemer's Adventures

JANE VH HEMBREE

ISBN-13: 9780692809808
ISBN-10: 0692809805

Beemer came to live with his human family when he was only seven weeks old. He soon learned that their names were Mom and Dad.

At first, Beemer was a little shy with his new family.

But, soon after he came to his new home, it snowed. Mom and Dad took Beemer outside to see what was coming down from the sky. He had not seen snow before and was a little puzzled.

"What is this white stuff?"

He ran and ran. Beemer looked like an airplane when he ran!

He loved the snow flakes. They froze his nose.

He wanted someone to come play with his softball.

Beemer chased the snowflakes.
He imagined that they were bugs he had to catch. Beemer had a really **BIG** imagination. When it was time to go in he said, "Oh, Mom, do I have to?"

Beemer didn't want to go in the house.

One day, a new friend came to Beemer's house. His mom
said that her name was Baby.
Baby and Beemer became very good friends.
They played together and took naps together.

Beemer and Baby

They loved to play on Mom and Dad's bed.

They pretended the bed was a boat and that they were floating on a bright, blue lake.

Sometimes Beemer and Baby would fall off the bed and that would make them laugh. Mom always said, "Now don't get hurt! That floor is hard." This made them laugh even harder. They would need help getting back on the bed.

When they got tired, they would try not to fall asleep. But sometimes Beemer fell asleep sitting up.

SHHHHHHHHHH !!

As the days went by, Beemer ran, jumped, took naps, played with Baby and grew...

AND
grew !

AND GREW !!

One day, Beemer and Baby went outside for a walk.
They loved going exploring in the yard.

Suddenly, they stopped! It was a turtle and they had not seen one before.

Beemer told the turtle that he had a friend whose name was Baby. He asked the turtle to be their friend. She was so happy because sometimes it was lonely in the woods.

They all played together for a long time.

Their favorite game was hide and seek. Slow
Poke always won.
She could hide her head in her shell and then pop out!

Beemer and Baby always laughed when she did this!.

Baby loved to hide in the flowers and Beemer had to find her. She asked Slow Poke to hide with her. Slow Poke had not played hide and seek before.

Beemer is having a hard time finding them.
Can you? Where are they? Beemer, Baby and Slow
Poke really know how to hide!

Beemer is looking and looking.

Beemer, Baby and Slow Poke had fun together and played until they were very tired. Baby and Beemer wanted Slow Poke to come home with them but she said she had to go because it was getting late. Her mother would be worried.

Good Bye!!!

Beemer and Baby wanted to visit Slow Poke and said they would ask Mom and Dad. Beemer was sure they would say yes. They were very sad to see Slow Poke leave.

Beemer and Baby will miss Slow Poke.

They came back to the house feeling very happy but tired. It had been a good day and tomorrow they might have another adventure. Beemer and Baby went right to sleep.

Sweet Dreams.

www.ingramcontent.com/pod-product-compliance
Lightning Source LLC
Chambersburg PA
CBHW042114040426
42448CB00003B/274